MOSQUITO & ANT:
POEMS

MOSQUITO & ANT

POEMS

KIMIKO HAHN

W. W. NORTON & COMPANY
New York · London

For information about permission to reproduce selections from this
book, write to Permissions, W. W. Norton & Company, Inc., 500 Fifth
Avenue, New York, NY 10110

The text of this book is composed in Fairfield Light
with the display set in Bernhard Modern and Futura Condensed Light
Composition by Platinum Manuscript Services
Manufacturing by Courier Companies, Inc.
Book design by Charlotte Staub

Library of Congress Cataloging-in-Publication Data

Hahn, Kimiko, 1955–
    Mosquito and ant : poems / by Kimiko Hahn
        p.   cm.
    ISBN 0-393-04732-6
    I. Title.
    PS3558.A32357M67   1999
    811' .54—dc21   98-41003
                                                            CIP

W. W. Norton & Company, Inc.
500 Fifth Avenue, New York, N.Y. 10110
http://www.wwnorton.com

W. W. Norton & Company Ltd.,
10 Coptic Street, London WC1A 1PU

1   2   3   4   5   6   7   8   9   0

for several of *the immortal sisters*

Carol Jud,

Meg Moss,

and

Tomie Hahn

Acknowledgments

For the writers whose words I take to heart, thanks to
John Weir, Walter Lew, Cornelius Eady, Joanna
Kiernan, Jessica Hagedorn, Marilyn Chin, Sharon
Kraus, Harold Schechter, Eileen Tabios, Moira
Egan, and, of course, Carolyn Lei-lanilau

Also, thanks to Jill Bialosky for her vision

To Miyako and Reiko Hannan for their tenacity

To Ted Hannan, for the unbearable heart

Some of these pieces have appeared in *Asian/
Pacific American Journal, Brooklyn Review, X-Connect,
Luna, Kenyon Review, Mānoa, Muae, Black Lightning,
TriQuarterly Review.*

I am grateful for a PSC-CUNY summer grant that
permitted some time to revise this manuscript.

Contents

We cannot be polite and attentive enough
For your heart to feel briefly relieved and happy.

—sung by Gao Xinsian
translated from Nu Shu by Carolyn Lei-lanilau

Speaking, writing, and discoursing are not mere acts of communication; they are above all acts of compulsion. Please follow me. Trust me, for deep feeling and understanding require total committment.

—Trinh T. Minh-ha, *Woman Native Other*

The Razor

I want to return to the moment
father and I brought the canister of mother's ashes
to the temple in some odd shopping bag.
We then dropped off the remains
to leave for a couple slices down the block
but the reverend pulled a robe
over her jeans and blouse,
picked up prayer beads
and suggested which was not a question
we say a sutra. Which one was it?
I only recall I didn't have a tissue;
that the incense which I so dislike
felt sweet wafting into my sweater
and hair; that my whole body
shook without pause
though I did not make a sound
and tears and mucus covered my face and
sleeves because father did not know
I needed the handkerchief
mother had pressed a week earlier.
At times the loss felt like an organ
one could excise with a razor.

Wax

Initial Correspondence to L . . .

i.
I am looking for clues
on how to stay a woman, not
a middle-aged woman
who sings all those girl-group lyrics
over the dash
but a woman since
I've earned that title
over years of (honey, you know—)
wicked repartees
among my girlfriends and boyfriends.
Here's the subtext:
the twenty-year-olds
at poetry readings
are so exquisite they might be
fashioned of wax, even
the blemishes. I realize now
how lithe I was when I thought
I was the ugly daughter—how
tremulous my beauty. I didn't know.
I just knew
I wanted to fuck my professor
(Chaucer 8:30 am M/W)
and boys from Chinese History
wearing blue caps. Nixon
was still President.
The war was nearly over.
And the young now listen
to fifty-year-old rockers.
No wonder they don't think
they invented sex. Fuckin-A
we did.

And what I want at some moment
in my forties
is not an affair—
that would rip my breast open—
I would like to wrap my arms around a guy
(I guess a guy)
for a lengthy kiss.
Standing up. In the dark.
Pulse at the boiling point
one recalls
from those irretrievable initial encounters.
L, send me advice quick.

ii.
waxing

iii.
I send these words to you
across the frozen continent,
through waning light
and steam rising off rivers.

Morning Light

But this one *does not exist.*

—Irigaray

The ceiling fan whisks the fatigue and camouflages the night silence. He is tired of being tired. She feels tired of the air. His body flinches as the muscles release the day: the students, the quizzes, the bag lunches. She feels he is letting go of her. That every night he lets go more but returns even before the alarm.

He *returns* for their daughters: to place bowls of cereal before their pouting faces still puffy with dreams. They squabble over who will read the cereal box while eating, who will get to do the maze and save the box top for the free disposable camera. Their hair dips into the milk. She is still in bed and listens. She imagines him reading the paper and drinking coffee.

He drinks his coffee black. Stands at the sticky counter and reads the news. Every surface is always sooty from the air blowing through the window. The building next door never cleans its incinerator. The girls' bickering inspires the dog to whine. Her robe is draped in a draft and feels cool to the touch.

Before she wraps her flannel robe around her fleshy body she stands sideways in front of the full-length mirror. Scowls at the stomach she can *see.* But she looks good *for forty* her daughters comment. *For any age,* she corrects. The air shivers across her. She hears him call, "I'm leaving."

She also hears the girls quiet as he turns on "The Road Runner" and takes the cereal box away. "See," the older one snaps. "I'm leaving," he repeats in the direction of the bedroom. She walks in to see him out.

The air blowing in from outside smells like ozone. She looks at their transfixed daughters. They will need to dress, brush hair, brush teeth in fifteen minutes. She takes out cold cuts and plastic wrap. She warns them, "I'm turning the TV off after this episode." Before pressing *off* she glances at the paper she will not read till lunch at her desk. *No Partial Birth Abortions,* she notices. They are not *partial births.* She gets angry. She puts it down and turns off the TV. The two complain, "The show isn't over." She replies, "It is for you two."

Ten years ago she thought she was losing pregnancy weight too slowly, that she was too unknowledgeable of current events,— that she was to blame for his disinterest. She didn't know that his reading the paper, say, had little to do with his waking hours. She tries untangling the oldest's hair, matted at the neck from a week of brushing her own hair for two seconds each morning. The younger one stands by her elbow as always.

"Why do you always interrupt me whenever I'm reading?" he had asked the night before. When can we talk—she wondered but had not said anything. Instead she had climbed onto his lap. He kissed her lightly and urged her off. "Love me?" she provoked. "Why must you ask?" She got up, went into the bathroom and looked at her face in the mirror, then closed her eyes.

She doesn't know when he closes his eyes he is shooting a BB gun at his brother's forehead or rolling his father's new compact. That his mother is telling him the body is ugly even as she rises out of the tub and reaches for a white towel she's heated on the radiator. "Feels so toasty," she had said. He had smiled and tried not to look at the patches of bubbles clinging to her blond skin. That summer he tried to bury her Pekinese alive.

She feels buried: that there is no feeling left in her body only the idea of feelings. She can't remember the last time her mouth watered for something like Godiva chocolates.

"Don't eat chocolate. You'll get fat and pimply," her father had warned her when she had come in from baby-sitting chewing a Mars bar. "No more peanut butter either." She was *already fat* and her skin and hair always oily. She felt dirty all the time. She was eleven. Already chocolate was connected to pain.

"Don't eat chocolates," she tells her oldest as she gives her spending money. Then, "Well, once a week is okay." And pulls her hair back gently. "Tie it back—there's another lice outbreak." The youngest is at her elbow with several elastic bands. "I want the red one—" the oldest begins. "No, it's mine," comes the other's correction. She warns them, "Don't start."

He'd forgotten the car radio and buzzes back in then starts to leave again. He looks handsome in his black denim jacket. When they first met at a demonstration she'd wondered why he was attracted to her. She had asked him on a walk along the Hudson with her dog. He kissed her deeply. She was already pregnant though neither knew and that news would be thrilling—desire and want clearly tangent.

Sometimes she wants to tell him: *why don't you just pack your trashy novel and toothbrush and fucking leave.* That's what she thinks now as she looks in the mirror. "Come on mom," she hears from the hallway. The girls can cross the street to the school by themselves this morning. She is running late.

When are they not late? After they leave with their kisses and lunches she pulls on a purple knit dress, black stockings and pumps. Lipstick later. She leashes the dog and as she steps out the door forgets the keys.

Kafka's Erection

i.

Dearest L, my lovely older sister,
I suggest to *you* what to say
to a former lover?
With two children my own longing often
feels alien—
the breast for nursing, the genitals
for birth (forget conception—).
As my daughters lose teeth, wear increasingly
sheer blouses, pierce their bodies—
learn to say *fuck you* in the school yard
—I am more *the older woman* each day.
As for *your* lover—well
I would probably seat him for lunch
loop around behind him
and lean close to his face—
so close there is barely air between.
Then see what happens.

ii.

My husband wants to know why
I carry your poems around with me.
As if a cashmere scarf. Or an air tank.

iii.

In infancy we travel from *mama* to *no*.
Then? A round-trip?

iv.

I scribbled a ten-page letter to you months ago.
It is folded on my nightstand among bills and bracelets.
And Kafka.

v.

I imagine us swimming to a sand bar.

vi.

Tell me what I should do
with all the black slips
purchased at thrift shops.
I mean to wear them as dresses.

Reflections Off White
for M

The werewolf is on. During her sister's wedding reception May and I curl up in the minister's cottage on a bed larger than my parents'. A sunny room with strict shadows. White chenille spread. The bumpy texture presses designs onto our legs. We are seeing a horror movie for the first time. Is it 1962? Is it before color?

May's first wedding is in Colorado. I am in a purple dress. She wears a creamy lace dress. On the plane home a rock star tries to pick me up but I don't recognize him and squint at his lines.

I am a bridesmaid. I have watched all Pia's plans from registering at Bloomingdale's to meals apropos for early evening. An Italian American, she marries in the original St. Patrick's on Prince Strawberry-gold bands. Before the year is out they will shatter all their dishes against the wall.

My first wedding: a white moire taffeta strapless gown with short jacket. Even his great-grandmother attends. I don't remember the cake—white with yellow roses? I decide not to keep the album after we split up. Only five photos—none with the cake. In one his mother smiles at him.

My second wedding I am three-months pregnant and drink only one glass of champagne which I throw up.

My sister marries a musician. My eighteen-month-old daughter wears a pink sailor dress and cheap red "patent leather" slippers. There are several bowls with ice and the shrimp our parents shelled all the night before. Even their hands look pink. I don't recall the music.

At my first husband's second marriage I wear a small black dress and red fishnets. He wins a bet with an office mate who figured I wouldn't show up.

My husband's coworker's niece's wedding is at The Sacred Blood Church in El Barrio. We don't know her. I weep when we all throw rice on the front steps. Her bridesmaids are all in peach.

At our close friend's wedding before he came out the music is mostly R & B. Several of the gay men comment on the pity of it. One wears an immaculate shark-skin suit and shades.

A friend calls to say she's eloped with her sweetheart so as not to deal with family. They go to City Hall then rent a car and drive to a bed and breakfast. The room smells of cedar. In the morning in the empty parlor there appears cranberry juice, cranberry muffins and tea all in glassware. The juice looks like blood. They never see only hear other guests.

My haircutter's mother designs the gown and has her grandmother's tailor in Red Hook sew it. He has cataracts but produces a terrifyingly delicate dress. She knows she will save it like a flower pressed in a Bible. She wears white roses in her hair.

A barkeeper you know wants to save her virginity for the wedding night. Her boyfriend tells her it doesn't count if he doesn't come inside her.

A friend's teenage daughter studies bride magazines: from the veils to the satin pumps. She wants to fall in love to marry. She wants everyone to turn as she enters the church with her father. She wants everyone to cry, especially her mother. She wants the groom to sweep the veil back and kiss her so hard her back bends.

A colleague marries in her fiancé's—in *their* apartment. They look like an immigrant couple, he in pinstripes and she in antique lace. Standing beside two poets I weep during the whole ceremony. The couple stands by the window and back lit by the mid-afternoon light, the groom doesn't have a face.

Note on Thematic Redundancy in Women's Verse, No. One

While she sews the back hem of his coat
before he swerves
into the suited traffic
he sits back at the breakfast table
and she recounts yesterday's errands
but cannot penetrate
the news that smudges off
on his fingers as he smoothes out
each page
and tells her *I'm trying to read.*

Mosquito and Ant

i.

The Immortal Sisters:
One has only daughters.
One has a husband and lover.
One has two ex-husbands.
One has a rock band.
One doesn't give a shit.
One has a lover fourteen years younger.
One is losing her lover.
One is losing her lover to breast cancer.
One writes on her coffee breaks at a bilingual program.
One circles an island in her station wagon.
One's first son just shot himself.
One wants a donor egg.
One tattoos fireflies on her back.
One can't speak to the others.
One searches for the others as her source of immortality.

ii.

At the cafe with pink marble tables
I imagine you still asleep, a profile
across the continent that darkens
from this ocean to your own.
Fish pierce the surface for gnats.
Seals twist and turn.
Perhaps you stayed up late
rereading *reptiles of the mind*
or *moths of consciousness*. Perhaps
you wrote a letter.
I'm trying to write
while a child repeatedly asks
if bleeding hurts.
Your oldest daughter

asks what her name *means*
and perhaps you think of
a day you asked your mother the same.
My mother is dead
and yours is living.
You tell me:
She still cooks for herself
and when I visit she talks to me
as if she's talking to herself.
Or was that my mother?
This correspondence blossoms like sea anemone
ingesting the krill of our hearts.

iii.

She
Shi in Japanese: four, poem, death.

In Chinese?
In *mosquito and ant* script?

(*Yes* in Chinese, yes.)

iv.

I want my letters to resemble
tiny ants scrawled across this page.
They spy a crumb of dark sugar
on the far side of the embankment
and their strategy is simple:
the shortest distance between two points
is tenacity not seduction.

I want my letters to imitate
mosquitoes as they loop
around the earlobe with their noise:
the impossible task of slapping one

across its erratically slow travel.
Those spiderlike legs. The sheaths of wings.
The body that transports disease.
I wonder if a straight man can read such lines.

I want my letters to resemble the smoke
when the widower burned his young wife's poems
so she might polish them in heaven.
The smoke not unlike that from burnt toast or punk.

Jam

on events in between correspondence to L

i.

He tells me I better not
be fooling around
as I lick capuccino froth
off a plastic lid. He tells me
he knows what's up
then wonders out loud
if a friend is
screwing around.
I tell him she
may be manipulative
but not so devious as to
complain she's not getting any
while she's getting some
on the side. I am
that devious
but if I were I wouldn't
be telling him. He
grins and says
yeah right. Tosses his cup
into the trash
and puts his hand
on the small of my back. He says
he knows
what's going on. Which, I say,
is nothing as long as you're supplying
the jam.

ii.

He tells me not to drink alone
and I tell him, I'm not. I'm writing
to her. He tells me

the same the next evening as he turns on
the News. I miss my self.
Dear L, you tell me I count on him
to retrieve my own body.

iii.

jam, jelly, preserves,—

iv.

He turns on the 7 o'clock news. He
reads the paper's Final Edition. He turns on
the 11 o'clock news. He reads
a spy thriller. He turns in.

v.

I tell him, Remember how
the wind blew spray
off the crests of waves? How
some nights our footprints
were phosphorescent?
And he says, What?

vi.

Meanwhile I read how female adepts
found students. I read how many
considered these women as *travelers*
from another dimension. I read
these chapters on the Immortal Sisters
and my fingertips tingle
as if catching breath.
My blood quickens as if to rip tide.

The Tumbler

i.

I call you.
I pour one then while on the phone
pour more
rum over a tumbler of ice cubes.
I call you
to hear your voice:
if you received the poems,
to tell you sorry I lost your essay.
To hear you ask if
I am giving to others
the tendrils I should be giving myself.
I call to hear you
tell me you love me
though you say so to everyone.
There.

ii.

You think wisteria
is a vine
that climbs hardy trees
in suburban gardens
and gridded parks:
then down the street you see a whole tree
with the fruitlike blossoms.
Do you know what I am saying?

iii.

You say you are curious
about what my new poems are "about."
I write this:
I've hardly eaten
for a week

and realize I need the hunger pangs
to match the longing for some thing—maybe
to sleep in your basement again,
maybe for that kid lingering on the corner,
cigarette hanging from the pouting lip.
Most likely the nicotine itself.
Even the second-hand smoke.

iv.

X sends a card—
he writes he cannot sleep because I am
on his mind.
And I imagine when he does fall out
I am just rising and pulling a slip over my shoulders.
I can almost hear the ivy clinging to the stucco.

v.

You think morning glories open
because you open
in that light
where we see so clearly
a coat tree, a box of old magazines,
a child's pull-toy caterpillar.
And they do.

vi.

You think I am ripped open
to the moon's movements.
And you are right.

Pine

i.

I thought wearing an evergreen dress
might be enough to express the longing
of the pine
though it or because it retains its scent
throughout the snowfall
and above the tree line. That's what I thought.

ii.

I needle my students
and a few write inflamed poems
to my ideological bent and my ankle bracelet.
I lay awake in the neighbor's light
through the curtain of flurries
we find in the real morning—
the one with real light.
And the only way to guide them
through their own compost
is to needle them harder—
to make them work not for me
but for the spruce
scraping at their windows. Still
X sends terrifying love letters
that send so much blood to the chest
the fingers are cold.

iii.

You say it's from *a crush*.

iv.

You say quit using these *he* and *hims*
when the specificity of *John*
is more engaging.
I needle: make me feel.

v.

Next time I make a C-note
from a poem
I will send you a red dress
I have tried on myself first.
The silk, light as the lotion
on the nape of your neck.

vi.

silk, rayon, chiffon,

vii.

You say it's the *he* in *heat*.

viii.

I see pine and I see
what I know is feeling.
I imagine stepping barefoot
under those trees
onto a bed of their
brown needles.
So prick my skin.

Note on Thematic Redundancy in Women's Verse, No. Two

Neither cognac nor tea will stall
what a run through the blizzard
suggests: by the corner pay phone
the heart throbs publically.
The men from the pizzeria
toss pie dough
and watch snow collect
inside my pulled-back hood.
They grin.
I listen to the answering machine
answer for him
and though he is listening
I do not leave a message
about lilies.

女

Translating Ancient Lines
into the Vernacular

I want to go where the hysteric resides,
the spinning a child knows
when she twirls around till air and earth
are inebriated and she falls
even bruises her knees even
as a delightful lake of sandwich and milk rises—
and she laughs so fully
the others laugh with her
or tell her:
now that's enough.

Zinc

i.

The script is useful.
I can love you,
even express the letters.
The stationery does not need fragrance because
the words fill
the air like dust motes circling
above the blankets this morning,
never to fall.

ii.

I mistook the tomato
for a vegetable.

iii.

I mistook my husband's back
for metaphor.

iv.

I mistook my desire to merge
for simple algebra
when that need is really *cosmic*.

v.

COMIC

vi.

You are translating *The Immortal Sisters*
back into Chinese.
To test the translation
and try your hand.
Staying up with dictionaries and charts
you forget the hour

and in your morning shower feel drunk-tired.
I know you.

vii.

Take zinc.

viii.

Bake me sweets.
Eat them and send the recipe.
Darling.

ix.

I received your postcard from a Chinatown coffee
shop:
Take your temperature.
Take your time.
Ditto the zinc.

x.

The problem is delirium
is addictive—
and infectious.

xi.

X and I finally remind one another
of what is not available
and what is: hedges, rose, pine.

xii.

I mistook pronouns
for tissue.

The Downpour

a zuihitsu *after Sei Shōnagon*

We do not know her name. We call her Sei Shōnagon. Shōnagon for her own palace title, "Minor Counsellor"; Sei, a character from her father's clan name, Kiyowara. We do not know her name. But she is not anonymous. Recent research suggests her given name may have been Nagiko. But we do not know her name just as we do not know the name of her contemporary and literary rival, Murasaki Shikibu. We do not know her name though it seems she was married to Tachibana no Norimitsu and may have had a son. On the other hand, neither may be true.

.

I love to hear a man talk while making love—not too much of course. I love to hear what he'd like to do or to have done. However the atmosphere is flattened if the man has flem in his throat and instead of gently coughing he gurgles on. Or if the man says he's going to come soon and really does. How boring.

.

If a man has a bit of a belly it's okay. But he should pull his belt down below it, not pretend it doesn't exist and buckle over it. No one wants to look matronly.

.

We do not know her name despite her influence in court and literature, despite the influence women held in court when men continued writing Chinese verse in Chinese using Chinese images; while women, prohibited from learning Chinese, wrote in the vernacular, in the language of their islands. They wrote in the childlike *kana* I first learned to write *Kimi*; in the only kana my grandma knew.

.

Ono no Komachi, Lady Ise, Murasaki Shikibu, Sei Shōnagon, Izumi Shikibu . . .

.

The language invigorated the literature, made the bloodless literature flush, and was so dominated by women, their sensibility became the aesthetic. Some men wrote in the female persona. And men of any worth became tainted by their radiant influence.

·

I despise a woman who cannot carry on a conversation but out of some neurosis chatters on, whether on international affairs or catchment areas, just like an adolescent boy talking about baseball.

·

A Marxist scholar who has praised my work, both poetry and politics, cannot fathom my undying attraction to Heian culture, the apex of the aristocracy where women were not allowed to be seen by any man except her father and husband though she may have affairs. Where a woman must speak to men from behind a screen though she may own property. Where the men powdered their faces and spent a great deal of time concocting perfume just so. *It's no more than a cult of beauty for the ruling class*, he noted. But the power of women's poetry inspires me like an older sister lending me a lipstick.

·

We do not know her name.

·

A student in my *Tale of Genji* class rightly noted how annoying it is when men do not flip up the toilet seat and spray it, or do not put the seat down after urinating. I asked her what that annoyance was really about. *Oh, their control*, she replied without hesitation. Yes, very tacky. Almost as bad as a lover lying down beside you and, placing his hands behind his head, opens arm pits in your face.

·

Yet, there is something comforting in the kind of sweat that smells like burning rubber.

·

Do we need to know her name.

There is nothing like changing the clock forward in spring and suddenly noticing, as if for the first time, leaves delicate as blossoms, insistent in the urban blight. Persistent as a child's bedtime request for water.

•

Much as I dislike cars, especially large ones, the mint Caddy with whitewall tires pulling out as I walked the dog this morning was so pristine I could well imagine myself in the passenger seat, stretching my legs out, pulling my cashmere coat around me.

•

I knew I had met my match when he returned from a tour and presented a lovely second-hand cashmere coat in perfect condition. He could read in my expression that I wanted to see other men but I couldn't broach it because of the gift. I waited a few days then told him, but in those few days he campaigned against such an arrangement and left me with little real enthusiasm for anyone else. What kisses in those early months! What a fragile thing is courtship, almost unidentifiable, even in this post-free-love era.

•

Her name, we do not know her name.

•

Before falling asleep last night I described this writing project to Ted: *There's a woman whose book was published a century ago—a kind of miscellany of likes, dislikes and observations. I've decided to write my own. Too bad she was such a bitch.* A few minutes later he asked, *Did you say it was written a thousand years ago? I thought it was by someone you know.*

The translator of the Penguin edition, Ivan Morris, notes that *The Pillow Book* is "a model of linguistic purity . . . [with] hardly a single Chinese word of locution in the entire book." (*PB*, 11)

•

Murasaki Shikibu wrote in her diary: *Sei Shōnagon has the most extraordinary air of self-satisfaction. Yet, if we stop to examine those Chinese writings of hers that she so presumptuously scatters about the place, we find that they are full of imperfections. Someone who makes such an effort to be different from others is bound to fall in people's esteem, and I can only think that her future will be a hard one. She is a gifted woman, to be sure. Yet, if one gives free rein to one's emotions even under the most appropriate circumstances, if one has to sample each interesting thing that comes along, people are bound to regard one as frivolous. And how can things turn out well for such as woman?* (PB, 10)

•

When he was first interested in me he didn't know how quickly poets can snap and I am particularly good. One evening on our way back to his apartment he said, "Every subway stop reminds me of a different girlfriend." That put me out and I told him so. But he continued teasing he had a "spare tire" somewhere. I replied, "Honey, you're off the road without a jack."

•

It's a pity wearing black is so trendy. It's so convenient to slip into black jeans and turtlenecks. And the clothes fade exquisitely into varied shades. One can appear vaguely hip without fussing.

•

Reading about the Empress's dog Okimaro I think of a story I heard from a fellow secretary. She saw a car door open and a dog pushed out just before it sped off. She wanted to take the poor thing to her apartment but already had three. Sei Shōnagon wouldn't have thought it, but it is a real metaphor for her times and our own roboticized phase of capitalism.

•

As with the daring poet, Ono no Komachi, Sei Shōnagon was reputed to experience a downfall: dying in squalor, unloved and desolate. Such a rendition is most likely a revision of her life by over enthusiastic Buddhists, eager for female repentance.

•

Hateful Things:
crumbs or grease on margarine
static electricity
buying a cup of coffee and finding it lukewarm

a woman who loses all her pregnancy weight in a few months
men who pass by saying, "sit on my face, China"
heads of state who create policies in the name of a god
mediocre writers who review books
discovering an artist one greatly admires is an elitist bitch

    •

A list of categories by her translator:
Things that make one's heart beat faster
Things that arouse a fond memory of the past
Oxen should have very small foreheads
A preacher ought to be good-looking
It is so stiflingly hot

    •

Considering the literary history of the rose I think of my own. My first husband and I had separated, my lover (or was I *his* lover?) had left for grad school and my interest, as those in monopoly capitalism, was to diversify. But the lover, especially isolated in a new city, could not let go as I needed him to. As I needed to. He sent me a rose every week. All the other secretaries envied the emphatic declaration. At first I was frustrated. I knew his meager fellowship did not allow for such extravagance. Then I began saving the buds. I found the small cellophane-wrapped collection the other day. Still red. Still a signal I love him. It's just as a friend told me after her divorce: *It's a fortunate person who experiences a grand passion in their lifetime.* The love is emblematic of loss and desire and ultimately even greater than the love object.

    •

The aristocracy during the Heian Period cut themselves off from foreign influence as well as real provincial government. They basked in high forms of indulgence. They created an art out of marrying one's cousin. They did not know the rough, hairy, unpowdered, unperfumed, warrior class outside the capital would cut them down.

    •

Women would never again enjoy the prominence, though limited to the aristocracy, they reached during the Heian Period. In the following eras, the samurai class dominated with an aesthetic diametrically opposed to the female sensibility, though the sense of melancholy and transience persisted through Buddhism. In fact women were regarded as vessels for the patriarchy, homosexual relations preferable to one with *a demon*.

•

D was returning to the U.K. with his "wife" who was still married to his best friend. The couple could not divorce though they had lived separately for half a dozen years. The husband was moving to London again so she moved. They all three had "open arrangements" so when D expressed an interest in me I felt no qualms. But she felt threatened he would use me as an excuse to remain in New York. I felt discarded and abused by their triangle, convenient only for themselves. *Bourgeois* they called people who questioned their liberated arrangement. I wanted him but wasn't that self-destructive. One afternoon I located him on scaffolding fourteen floors up the side of a building. He waved a paintbrush when he recognized my down vest. Before he left New York he did spend a week with me.

•

When I see him now I recall kissing in a downpour beneath the eaves of a warehouse. Our Nikes soaked. Utterly Romantic.

•

Forbidden to see their faces the men would fetishize the calligraphy, paper, spray of flowers, memory of sleeves trailing beneath a screen or carriage door, perfume left in the wake of their attention.

•

We do not know her name.

The Akashi Woman Speaks
above a Whisper

Though she weighs ninety-five pounds
she apologizes when pulling off her jeans
because her body curves,
because she has breasts,
because she has fine hairs on her ass and knuckles.
Because her ass is shaped like a fan.
He takes her apology
pushes her against the white sheets
saying, *There. There you are.*
I was nineteen as I recall.

Garnet

i.

X wanted to present a gift
the husband would not detect
as inclination. Book bag.
Rhyming dictionary. Hand mirror.
I copied poems from *The Orchid Boat* for him.

ii.

You are the Empress Wu Tsu-T'ien
requesting her lover
examine her *pomegranate dress*.
I am as delighted as you.

iii.

Eating a bowl of raspberries
I imagine X sucking
on the beads of my garnet necklace—

iv.

She began as concubine to Emperor T'ai then to his son,
Emperor Kai, until he replaced his Empress with her. She ruled
China from that moment. After his death and into old age she
kept a male harem, concubines and courtier lovers. How do you
feel about this?

v.

nipples the color of garnet

vi.

You advise, why dull a sharp point?
why flatten the crests? why
rinse out color? why douse what
the gut claims from the heart—

vii.

the *he* residing in the *she*

viii.

garnet hard as nipples—

Chekov's Diner

i.

I haven't gotten to the Russians yet:
the snow banks, the blue hands,
the cells.
What I do know: bleaching cloth in the snow,
nettles, sand pits—you know,
the Japanese.

ii.

What about metaphors? *Radiator?*

iii.

a match striking a matchbook

iv.

sulpher

v.

What about the kiss?
Was it dry and light—
bites on the earlobe
and on the sideburns—
licks around the eyebrows—
a stray hair on your tongue—
did it mean when he kissed his mother in Taganrog
it would be a different act?

vi.

After-coffee kisses taste like the scent of skunk, X insists.

vii.

the speaking with a spray of cherry

viii.

5 7 5 7 7

ix.

Meet me after 7:00 by the news stand.
At the Express Mail Box.
By the uptown token booth.
Next to the phone at the laundromat.
Behind the diner.
On the corner of—

x.

incensed

"Guard the Jade Pass"

i.

I am in the middle of "The Fourteen Poems" by Sun Bu-er
("Clear and Calm Free Human"), Taoist and one of the Seven
Immortal Sisters who took up the Tao after she turned fifty-one,
after her three children grew up, after her husband attained
enlightenment—highly approved by The Complete Reality
School. She was born in 1124. Commentary by Chen Yingning
of the twelfth century. Translated by Thomas Clearly. Copyright
1989. The Chinese is not included.

ii.

Some of the titles:
Gathering the Mind
Nurturing Energy
Cutting Off the Dragon
The Womb Breath
Facing a Wall

iii.

Imagine words with a dimension
not unlike the light and dark regions
of the moon. The back of planets. The crators.
Words that orbit the body
like a plea granted.

iv.

I am in the middle of—
what do you call this *pass*?

v.

When I am unblocked,
not in the midst of students and professors,

I walk around light-headed
as if there is too much oxygen
in the air.
Who needs sleep or water—

vi.

in the middle of—

vii.

The secret texts may reveal how to really be alive. Those by Sun
Bu-er are said to have been handed on by revered Taoists; one of
whom was known as the "Realized One of Mount Heng."

viii.

I keep a cigar box
on my bureau and fill it with objects
befitting a private altar:
coins, feather, thread.
An empty envelope when you forget
to enclose the letter.

Orchid Root

i.

Who thinks of the orchid root
but the horticulturalist
or the one now holding shears
and a jar of water.
Who thinks of the soil
but the gardener when
even the scent of mulch completes the air
like light.

ii.

my hands smelling like tobacco
from his shirt which smelled of my hand lotion

iii.

I need to return to the Chinese women poets.
The flat language
of pine and orchid.
The clouds playing over the crescent moon.
Return to the coy lines
that advertise and protest.
The words weighted in object
as much as flight.
If there was a bridge outside my window
I would slip on silk slippers
the ones with a phoenix
and run across
to the sisters who know
how to instruct the senses:
when to know the difference
between the narcissus fragrance
and burning rubber.

iv.

Take—the anonymous courtesan
who wrote the lines:
My hairpins on your fallen jacket—
My stockings on the tiles—
My petals on your root—

v.

The women write poems to one another
to protest the man's inattention:
and they fall in love
consequently
as the honeysuckle climbs the fence
from one garden to the next
its fragrance on the draft beneath the door.

vi.

PINE   杉

MAGPIE   鵲

CLOUD   雲

vii.

You and M can read classical Chinese
and I envy you both
like the bitch
I was raised to be:
haughty *and* self-effacing.
Always wanting.
Always evasive.
What saves me is my knowing
if I don't want to write about something
there is nothing else to write.
This is what compels me
to locate the characters in *Matthew's*.

viii.

the grass radicals—

ix.

Clearly I need the taste of plum
on my hands, my chin, his lips.
His. Mine. Plumb.

A Boat down the River of Yellow Silt

The first box held tiny yellow apples
from the tree behind your home.
Now inside the vestibule
a brown box with *mochi, manju,*
and a persimmon
like the hearts of various creatures.
I will eat one sweet tonight, one tomorrow
and after the ripening
on the sill that corners the morning sun
as we leave for the world
I will eat the one you tended yourself:
slice it open and lick the dark halves
that nourish its oval pit—I will
suck out these plump tongues of fruit
that speak for you.

Radiator

i.

Any strong sensation is a welcome break
from oxygen—

ii.

horse manure outside the stable
cigar smoke saturating the train seats
steamed asparagus from the steamer

iii.

I am not sure what I want
except that he wants
much the same: coal, flint, radiator.
But is X more
of my heart than my heart?

iv.

Any sensation penetrates my skin.
The cold porcelain tub,
the splintered deck,—

v.

X could last into the first snowfall,
the predicted blizzard.
And no you don't, I think to tell him,
wish I was your girlfriend.

vi.

for the taste of his mouth:
the acid of coffee and tobacco, the acid
of any initial encounter—

vii.

Dearest L, please advise—
for what thread could stitch the flesh
back into one piece—

Clippings

the mundane in between correspondence

i.

What I learned on this past trip:
Sexual tension is never disappointing.
There are black stingrays with white polka dots.
Coral is a type of anemone.
(Some somersault. Some move at a rate of four inches/hour.)
Lower one's expectations in men.
Some sexualize activities, some sublimate sexual energy.
$5/day parking behind The Art Institute.
Marxism is not dead.
We are not necessarily seeking sex so much as stimulation.
A can lead to B then become B.

ii.

Note to myself:
Forgot to mention in my last letter
how a friend's bird
is in love with a paper towel tube.
It fluffs its crown and wings,
struts of course,
then rubs its brow
and attempts to stick its head in the tube.

iii.

What I noticed on this past trip:
when I am away from you I feel homesick—
that feeling of nausea and hunger,
empty and full. Bleeding and bled.
Of missing a part of the body—
have you seen it?

iv.

Save clipping:
The cuscuta in Bryant Park
strangle then suck
the ivy in the northwest corner.
Also known as hell bind
and devil's sewing thread,
if the parasite sprout
does not find a host immediately
it creeps along,
the tip growing, the rear dying off,
till it finds something
to coil around.
Horticulturalists
advise gardeners to weed by hand
or spray MCPA or DCPA.

v.

Save clipping:
"Secret Life of Jupiter's Moons."
Their molten cores may allow
enough change
for life. We can see the cracks
on the bald surface
through the delighted telescope.

vi.

What I noticed this past hour—
the spirit nestles in the mundane
not the fantastic. So
I look in my bowl of cereal.
My basin of water.
A tank of clown fish.

Annotation in Her Last Court Diary

The before-snow sky lasted like the perpetual twilight
of a day when drinking might begin early
and extend an arm over the shoulder of the afternoon.
And, because not at the office,
one could lie across the bed fully clothed
and come once, twice, whatever.
Then what?

Lady Rokujō Hails a Taxi

In the early morning after she steps in
off the block of tourist bars
the taxi driver
takes a second look in the rearview mirror
to assess the narrative of her tousled clothing
and cheeks chafed by his rough face
as she lights up.
And the driver knows,
more than the passenger,
it is limitation
that holds each one in the desert
to enjoy feeling parched
because it is feeling.

Croissant

i.

love indelicately

ii.

did you know on the flight home
as the tip of the jet

lifted through the stratus weather
and into translation

before translation becomes language
I thought we might

on my flight home did you know

iii.

X provokes answers.
But I know I provoked the yeast,
the rising.

iv.

I drink cappucino at the bakery
eyeing the men in the back
with their great mixers
and stacks of tarts—
watch them carry pies to the oven
in their white aprons, shorts and sneakers.
One in particular breaks
to light up outside
in the sun. I've been a woman
as long as he's been alive.
He winks.
He says, *Hey darling. Did you get a warm one?*

v.

One clipped hair from my already short cut
and sealed it behind his driver's license—
a dozen years ago. And now?

vi.

despite the tarmac

vii.

I lean close to X, over his shoulder
into an anthology of the Beats,
to notice the pierced ear
he no longer adorns.
How would it look with
a purple ridge of teeth marks?

viii.

Two years ago I told my oldest, when asked—
that, yes, a man puts his penis
in the woman's vagina—
thinking this is what I wasn't told.
We both made a face.
It sounded so silly and slimy.
It was good she asked to know.

ix.

on my flight home—

x.

A woman photographs me
for a magazine.
She explains to my daughters
about light and chemicals.
About the iris.
We all fall in love with her.

xi.

the immoral sisters

A Late Entry in the
First Wife's Pillow Book

How can I know my glance can
echo in a man's chest cavity? How can
I know my chatter over coffee
can abduct brain cells?
That a man might say
or a woman—
this is important. This caffeine
you call you.
This afternoon. This stunning taste
so otherwise absent in these hallways?
This pressure—as I turn toward the open window
away from everyone's soiled laundry?
Where can I realize it is still possible
to provoke a heat clear
as cold air?

The Lunar Calendar
She Pins to the Door

Why spend love? Why
make available
a narrative that evaporates
like rubbing alcohol on cotton?
Do I strategize against wound
even as I head full tilt?
If I lie on my back
and breathe the air
the trees in the courtyard
expire into the window
perhaps I may stop *forgetting myself*,
quit looking for some other
to locate my own body.
What I do find after coming alone
is if I press my ear flat to the bed
I can hear my heartbeat
in the springs of the mattress deeply.
On your own, you write to me.
Mortal and stunningly adequate.

The Intelligentsia of the Chin
Dynasty Desire Desire

I sit near the back of the pastry shop
where I first began to sort my thoughts on L.
To correspond
with pulse and impulse.
Now there's snow.
And empty boxes that contained first apples
then fat persimmons
from L's small backyard—
the persimmon tree planted
by her first husband
did not bear fruit until after he left
and she ripped it from the soil,
transferred it to the solitary patch of sun.
From that same tree she sent me three,
twig and leaves still attached
not to prove authenticity
but to suggest the Chinese brushstrokes
one recalls from girlhood lessons
sitting on knees till feeling is absent
and the calligraphy generously exact.

Tissue

I want to return to the high chair
in the terrace's noon sun—
the cat slipping between legs, the fern seeking shade.
Every thing is sharp and shiny.
The air smells like a pleased cry.
I want to see my mother's face become radiant
when she turns away from the stove to me.
To touch me with her lips,
red against everything yellow.
Her cool hands to take me somewhere with her.
I want that to never end but it ends

constantly—play here, bye-bye, here's dada, no no, night-night.
It ends like a cry ends and the air is not a color
but blank like a monitor. No blanker.
Not even a fallow garden but a bed. Not a bed
but a wall.
Not a wall but a door the student avoids
it is so close to the gut.
Not a door but a heart.

A fist. Focusing on her own fist
at some point the baby knows it is attached
and she can move it, say, to her mouth.
The fist feels good, tastes vaguely *like mother*.
The nipple. The Other.
Mother, you have been exiled

by narrative and death so long
I forgot your heartbeat
until I leaned against my daughter's tiny chest,
heard the beat the baby mistakes for the whole world.
The heart inside the body the way the baby
was inside this body.

Chuang Tzu's Mistress
Sleeps in a Draft

She dreams she leans over the brown dust
and lifts a brown leaf that is a moth,
holds it inside her mouth
to revive the flutter from a frost
now covering the still-live grass,
the fallen pears half eaten by deer,
and her shoulders exposed from the comforter
her lover always drags to his side of the mattress.
Or was it a monarch? she mutters.

Untitled

Isolate yourself. If they find out about you it's all over.
—MICHELLE CLIFF

She does not want the lizards to touch her
but she wants to look at them
on the screen of her grandma's house.
They are either still as a leaf
or so quick you think you
are not sure something was there at all.
She is four and likes to look at things
she has never seen before anywhere.
Breakfast is ready and it's cornflakes
or rice and fish.
Grandma's hands smell like cleanser.

On the continent in Des Moines
there was a man on a porch swing in July
who took the opportunity
to tell me about *Oriental girls*
in the Pacific Theater.
Or the guy in West Virginia who
thought I was miraculously
that *lounge girl* he met in Saigon, 1968.

Years earlier my great-grandmother would not admit
my parents through her front door.
My mother-in-law could barely attend
the wedding. My sister's childhood hair
was red as a stop sign.
Now the way my mother did not look like me
my own daughters also
do not look *like me*
unless I can look beyond *blond*
or *tall*. Or the skin of influence.

Perhaps the lizards know something
by staying on the outside of the screen
and almost blending
or fooling peripheral vision but not probably
other lizards. How many species are there—
how many if any cross over
in a green miscegenetic frenzy—ah!
And through the shadows of the room
with the lizards on the screen
incense from grandma's morning prayer to grandpa
wafts into everything. Even solid things.
Even your skin.

I knew different men before the husband—
an Asian the mother claimed I desired
because Asian. Perhaps.
After all his calling me *kimi*
or my calling him *anata* comforted.
And I watch, predatory, men who are mixed
though one knows how futile color can be.
In the heat of the island's heart

where there is no sea breeze to relieve
the sweltering yard
grandma collects the fruit no one picked
from the tree she says bears mango
you cannot eat though no one
ever thought to ask why.
I never thought to ask, *dōshte obāsan?*
Dōshte taberarenaino?
And it has nothing to do with those lizards
or the headless chicken
on the counter in the too-hot kitchen.

The New Calligraphy Tutor Is a Woman

One was punched in the mouth.

One was stripped and locked in her room.

One was slashed along her pregnant belly.
One was forced to suck off a screw.

When the daughter is told to leave the room
because she laughs so loudly at her brother
her food slips down her chin—
she wishes to tell every one
go fuck yourself
but instead lays down on the carpet in her room,
quiets then laughs until she weeps.

One was bayonetted.

One sits in the brimming bathtub
sloshing water onto the linoleum and singing too loudly.

She loves her own voice radiating off the tiles.

Responding to Light

i. *"Every desire has a relation to madness—* IRIGARAY (*10*)

In the house with windows that look out
into the branches of a forest, into
the dinner of sunsets,
no one is permitted to speak
over the five o'clock news and no one
can see the television but the father.
Here, the daughters chew the meal
that will make them larger than desired,
than desire itself. Here
the father's paycheck purchases the meat
the mother stews.
Here the silent daughters are silenced
like the undergrowth across the street.

In the house with the father's still lifes
of massive seashells and slippery marine life
the daughters imagine the canvases are windows
without blinds. When the two
leave for school on the road by the elms
the younger one asks about the gnarled branches
that grow away from air toward the water table.

And once a year the girls share small foiled hearts:
the taste of chocolate stimulating and simulating
what cannot be said though there are noises.

ii. *". . . our society and our culture operate
on the basis of an original matricide."* (*11*)

Somewhere in the small house with no hallways
the mother disappeared
just before the oldest daughter's plump body

too early sprouted hair
and too early, though any time was too early,
budded nipples. This daughter
already knew since third grade that she would bleed
and in the telling had shivered uncontrollably
as if there was no such thing as radiators.
If *I* had told her that early evening
I would have held her
and not let go. I would not have left.
When the girl finally did bleed
in her baggy cotton underpants
she stuffed them with toilet paper
then later hid them between wall and mattress.

SOAR
SORE
SOEUR
SOUR
SUR
SURE

The curtains were gauzy
because the street and neighbors were far
from viewing inside
the interior of the house that resembled
a heart without blood. Veins without color.

iii.   "... *the threatening womb. Threatening*
       because it is silent, perhaps?" (16)

The womb says things like
come here go away
or *go away come here,*
darling.

iv. *". . . corps-a-corps"* (*10*)

They peeled carrots.
They added and subtracted.
They traded blouses.
They were more daughters than sisters.
They trimmed each other's hair and pierced their faces.

v. *". . . sentences that translate the bond between*
our body, her body, the body of our daughter." (*18*)

If she touches her body in the gray bathroom
the gray light lighting the small window,
squeezes her nipple or flicks her vulva—
if she tastes her taste
she is tasting her mother and daughter.
On the Pacific shoreline the marine life crawls back
from the tidal pool or gives up
the desire to breathe underwater ever again.
If she touches herself she can
find that pulse that penetrates like an echo.
All this without sound in the gray light off the green tiles,
like the real waves on any shoreline. Even lakes.

vi. *"We barely . . . have access to fiction!"* (*10*)

The stories, even when told by father,
were mother's: the one about the shark
beyond the coral reef,
the poi in kindergarten, the red seaweed
washed onto the beach and collected for dinner—
these were her stories we listened to
in our own heads in the house
with rooms filled with the shadows of limbs.
And she never thought they were *important*.
She knew though we knew she didn't know

how they would become not only our stories
but the granddaughters' tales to tell classmates
in the school yard filled with balls and ropes.

So every time the daughter *sees* someone
she moves away from the rooms
that imitate the ventricles that are finally only tissue.
Every time she speaks it is a leave-taking
of the sealed-off room she knew existed all along
toward a stew fragrant with fiction.

Komachi to Shōshō on the Ninety-ninth Night

I will tell you what I am feeling:
the back of my knee
desires your tongue, my ass
your fingers,
my waist your palms, my clit
your rough chin,
my nipples your lips, my lips your teeth,
my earlobe
your teeth, my shoulder blades
your fingernails, my instep your toes, my
inner thighs your hips, my heart
your eyes.

Becoming the Mother

"The shamans turn themselves into birds; the tumblers into serpents; the madmen into stones."

—CATHERINE CLÉMENT

For Miyako and Reiko

She became a sink.
She became a blind.
She became a styrofoam coffee cup.
She became a ballpoint pen.
She became the breeze through the door's splinters.

·

She became the mother who was at work at work,
at work at home
and at work at the shore
so her children never saw her
without a pencil tucked behind her ear.

She became the mother
who copyedited at a tony house
before marrying and quitting *that nonsense*.

She became the mother
who began with her own
father father father.

She became the mother
tattooed with versions of virgins.

She became the mother
who never gave birth, never
adopted, never kidnapped
and whose biological clock
has been diffused.

She became the mother
she thought she had had.

She became the Other.

She became the mother who drank.

She became mother
of her girlfriend's child.

She became the mother
of any man who stepped
into the caffeine of her madness.

She became the mother
of betrayal.

She became the mother
who died in a hit-and-run.

She became the mother,
120 years old,
who eats a pound of chocolate a week.

She became the mother who is becoming.
In fact, stunning.

·

She had forgotten *how to speak*
especially to her husband
who for a dozen years
had nearly become the mother
she thought she had and had
before her sister was born.
The husband had adored her.
He had desired her desire.
He had honored her words
and even liked her voice at a mic
or in bed when the shade was drawn
to the draft
blowing from limbs outside to limbs inside.

Then she forgot. Her tongue
slept even when her mind sprinted.
Her teeth locked. Her lips
felt pasted shut.
When had he become that mother
who had left her so alone
when the baby cried?
When had his heart become that heart
withdrawing from the whorls of her offerings?

                    •

The daughter writes a story
for the teacher
and for her mother who is a poet.
The story is about
a neighbor boy and girl
whose parents all die suddenly
on an afternoon of rock climbing.
The story traces the adventures
of the two orphans
who search for someone
to adopt them.
After circumnavigation
they look up the boy's uncle in Canton
who they find has also died
but his wife takes them in as her own.
This is a true story of her story.

                    •

She became the mother who taught herself how to read
and was later tenured at a university
where she screwed the canon with radiant pleasure.

                    •

How do daughters rehearse departure?
In letters to ungrateful boys,
in dresses too expensive for papa,

in swimsuits too small for comfort,
in baking breads, in "achievement tests"?
In speaking with an aunt about bleeding?

     •

She became the mother heating stones
to tuck at the foot of her own bed
for the time being.

Sewing without Mother

a zuihitsu for my sister

As with tending a newborn, the days pass slowly, the months quickly. With each new season we all, even the littlest, recognize what mother has missed, and what we see through our loss, since she died over a year ago. Even the bamboo shoots that father digs up with the girls and parboils for us to take home. Mother had suggested it and now we eat them thinking—*how tender, how tender.*

I think of famous writers such as Bashō, Ki no Tsurayuki, Issa, Sei Shōnagon—Kamo no Chōmei's bubbles we read about in *bungo* class with Professor Varley, read even the annotations in Japanese. A decade ago. I am returning to the work now to see how they wrote diaries and miscellaneous entries. Particularly Issa's *Oraga haru.*

The elation and detail in Issa's book—even watching his wife count their daughter's flea bites as she's nursing—then his grief with the same attention.

I walk past a certain frame shop near the children's school just to see the proprietress who resembles mother. Her hair covers her cheeks as she leans over an Utamaro print. Like an Utamaro print.

The Issa journal becomes an anthology as he jots down other poems on grief.

I sometimes think my many years in graduate school were a waste, especially since I can no longer read Japanese with ease. And because the renown scholar with whom I wished to study really didn't give a damn about me. But recently, in thinking about the women who have been influential in my life, I remembered the professor who chose me as a research assistant for work on censorship in postwar Japan. I scoured the library and annotated dozens of books for her bibliography.

In Iowa City I baby-sat for my writing instructor who lived down the alley. In her bedroom I noticed several bottles of perfume and tested them at a local shop. One smelled *green* and was not too expensive. I wear it still.

Eighteen months after losing mother in a violent car accident our lives have spun on. Still, even in our apartment we hear the related terror as boys shout the brands of crack they're peddling.

Over a year now and I can travel and unpack my nightshirt, toothbrush and manuscript. I can stand at a hotel window and watch pedestrians flee a thundershower they thought would not cross their commute. Waves of rain flood the street. Traffic lights change for no one. Music videos block the hum of the building and the fact of strangers in the next room.

In July we have the dog "put down." Four months later our first parakeet dies within a day.

Miyako tells me grandmother's death is her fault. I do not understand what she does not understand.

Reiko asks Ted if the universe goes on forever. He says it does. She comments, *then it must be very big and now it's bigger because grandma is there.*

Miyako acts badly at dad's house. I realize she cannot bear the absence of mother sewing potholders, piecing together a puzzle, rolling out biscuit dough.

In a remote South East Asian society people view sudden death as an honor—that the goddess who gave them life, needing their assistance, summoned their presence. The deceased enjoy a modest sainthood for a period of seven weeks, a number associated with harvesting. I invent these rituals.

The entries in a typical Japanese journal are nature-oriented, a convention. The frost, maple, cherries. All exhibit what lies at a tangent to language. I think of the sound of straw under Bashō's head as he turned in his sleep.

The change of seasons brought fresh grief it's true, but in the second year I think: a year ago it was only a few months, or a year ago we were buying this birthday cake without her.

There are still several of her suits in father's hall closet. I keep promising to go through them but know I won't any time soon.

I imagine leaving our two-bedroom rent-stabilized apartment that transported me through a first marriage, divorce, romances, a second marriage, two pregnancies and births. Then waking for the phone at 2 am for that news that would change our lives forever: mother's death.

Earlene says the roots of one's behavior will not change, but one's relationship to it can be modified. Even radically. But what happens when a party to that behavior is missing?

Sometimes I become annoyed with mother's inabilities—the jealous streak I wasn't aware of but inherited, absorbed from her silence. Her shutting off instead of confronting.

A student said that if Genji is symbolically searching for his dead mother he must have felt abandoned as a child. That the parents' departure indicates this to the child.

I watch the aerobic instructor talk with her mother. Both wear unitards.

After a vigorous workout I lock the lavatory door and weep as if from physical fatigue.

If only I could read the texts again—but even my dictionary usage is rusty. Wish I could navigate the reference books. Wish I could read the annotations with ease. Wish I could read the *kanji* without counting the number of strokes in the radical.

As father describes her jealousy he describes a powerful emotion I never witnessed in her but wish I had. Any strong emotion.

Reclamation for the married ones may mean the spouse will become more "mother." For my father, that he will seek relationships with women. But for the children, who will provide them with the many missing pieces—a grandmother, part *mother*? Will they live with more loss than the adults? Will they grieve forever?

the taste of daikon

I see a book on Tibetan thought regarding reincarnation. I am tempted to purchase it. Perhaps there *are* a certain number of souls that circulate. Perhaps she is an infant, now learning to speak. To touch a mirror. A child with her own mother.

What did she think of herself?

I make up myths to comfort myself, give myself rites I do not possess.

I want father to continue grieving as an expression of my own pain and to pay for his arrogance toward mother. Interrupting her. Telling her she was wrong. Correcting her. Dismissing her opinion. Poking fun at her. Silencing her.

Sipping a beer he keeps me company while I cook. Corrects me with "kitchen tips."

Are our lives spiraling around if we retrieve our annoyances with one another? If we can take the risk?

We still haven't decided where to place her ashes, cannot think of a single place she might have liked. Maui still comes to mind. Or some body of water.

Did Ted and I begin the process of "resolution" when we viewed her body? Said good-bye to the body no longer "hers"? To believe she was dead?

How did we explain her death to ourselves? On one level an "accident." But a part of me believes the Japanese superstition that she was a substitute death for another loved one. She subverted fate.

A friend with two little boys tells us the older one wants to kiss her romantically. I tell her my daughter wants to kiss me romantically.

Are the boys in Lee's kindergarten class so raucous because they perceive her as Other? as the one whom they are not *like*?

Reiko is especially tired this evening. She cries hysterically as Ted walks out of the room. After twenty minutes I go in and ask her what's wrong? *Daddy took me into the kitchen but there is a red bucket. Then he carried me into my room but there are red letters on the circus poster. And the book he chose has a girl with a red dress. And my lost elephant was red and I'll never see it again.*

When she falls asleep where does she go?

The girls believe mother is *somewhere*. Even after one asks what I think and I give my cloud-sun-wind version, they still believe she is somewhere waiting for them, looking like she did when we saw her two days before the crash when we waved good-bye from the car and she turned to go back into the warm house.

The poet reading before me is slender. I am not as delicate and beckoning. My body is curvier partly from type, partly from a few extra pounds. Mother was slender but for a very round abdomen. Fibroids? I disliked her stomach. Yet, here is mine. As I recall her she was probably thirty-eight.

Several people have told me I will speak to her.

She loved to speak Italian. It must have been a cord to her years in Rome when everything was shiny and exquisite. And I was part of that time.

I am pleased with the girls' manners. *Yes, please*. And, *Fine, thank you*.

Miner defines a *zuihitsu* as *stray notes, expressing random thoughts in a casual manner . . . [Though some] do show a semblance of logical structure*. I am attracted to this semblance.

We finally find a co-op we like and the bank will approve. The building is a brownstone but white, not brown. We have a garden with a pink dogwood. We will watch it from the bedroom.

I have an envelope of seeds mother marked *marigolds*.

Ki no Tsurayuki saw the pebbles and recalled his deceased daughter playing in the sand.

I think of her more since she died but it isn't true. It's how I think of her.

Father says the *pillow book* is of an erotic nature but I can't find a citation to that effect. I can't even find a reference to its origin which I think was a little drawer in a boxlike *pillow*. Keene calls this form a *zuihitsu* in the introduction to his translation of *Tsurezuregusa. Zuihitsu:* free flowing brush.

In both Sei Shōnagon and Kenkō's work, the pieces are more discreet than my own which are often a cross between a journal entry and a sketch. I like the flow in my own structure but I also like the gemlike quality of the so-called essays.

a fan with the mother-of-pearl fallen out

When I fly on an airplane I wear her jade snowpea as a talisman—and possible means of identification.

Miya's best friend, who has seen a number of classmates leave the City, vows she will be the next to move *so I can break someone's heart.*

I am still not sure how to wind the bobbin of mother's machine—I'll need to wait for Tomie to return from Japan. I hope she will remember. Then I hope this antique will work.

To teach a course on the diary: Sei Shōnagōn, Kenkō, Bashō, Anaïs Nin, Samuel Pepys, the Alaskan woman a student mentioned, Anne Frank, Thoreau.

Why the diary? The immediacy of the record—the spontaneity. Also the artifice in the face of publication.

To teach them how to thread a needle, stitch and knot it.

a box of white buttons

Reiko says she wants to die when I die.

Keene: *The formlessness of the* zuihitsu *did not impede enjoyment by readers; indeed, they took pleasure not only in moving from one to another of the great variety of subjects treated but in tracing subtle links joining the successive episodes.*

Even my stories utilize the *zuihitsu* anti-structure.

I hear a toddler left with a sitter cry out: *mommy mommy*. An echo in my ribcage.

When he turns away from me in bed I feel my body disappear until all that's left is one thought: trying to turn abandonment into sleep.

Every day I want to call mother. Especially since dad has returned from his various trips. He tells me not an hour goes by that he doesn't think *of that woman*. Mother.

Ted asks what I want in my relationship with dad—but is that something I can even articulate? Perhaps I need to try.

Since mother died I have no one to whom I can really brag about the girls—who will now take pleasure in their small accomplishments.

The seminar is nearly halfway through *Genji*. They will be surprised when he dies before the book's end.

the black cherry blossoms

A boy about eleven kicks me as I exit a bus and I turn and shout at him. He shouts back and before I realize it, I've grabbed him by the jacket and pulled him out of the bus stairwell. I'm tired of taking shit.

I'm tired of taking shit.

He sees a red kimono and thinks of her.

I am suddenly struck by the intense interest mother had in reading Nin's diaries—I attributed it, at the time, to its offbeat quality and short entries. I never considered the way it was written, that is, as a means to re-create one's experiences. That she must have needed this kind of identifying and healing. I will look at the books differently now. I need to call dad to get them.

Can't seem to reach dad. The phone rings at least ten times.

I never knew about mother's intense jealousies. Her fabrications—just as I would fabricate jealousies in order to feel miserable. In order to feel.

Finally roast a turkey myself. Timid cook though I am I alter the stuffing to suit my taste: add chestnuts, apples and a teaspoon of curry.

A chartreuse circle skirt mother had pinned for hemming was draped on a chair when I arrived after the accident. It has hung on a chair in my bedroom now eighteen months. Forever. Not a long time at all.

blanket, arrowhead, cloud filling, herringbone, wheat-ear, Holbein, overcast, star filling, Vandyke, fly, fern, fishbone—

Miya wants to make sense of the loss so the world can make sense.

How to define ambition for oneself, apart from one's parents? Can a girl really use her father as a model?

I've given the girls potholder looms—the metal kind I had. I actually couldn't wait till they were old enough because I had enjoyed them. As usual, Reiko needs more attention; for Miyako it is a solitary activity.

Mother, Rei's feet are narrow and long like Ted's.

Notes

"The Razor." Triggering line: "Keeping in line an intimate celebration." Catherine Clément (35). From Hélène Cixous and Catherine Clément: *The Newly Born Woman*, translated by Betsy Wing, introduction by Sandra M. Gilbert (Minneapolis: University of Minnesota Press, 1986). Originally published in *Paris: La Jeune Née* by Union Générale d'Éditions, 1975.

"Mosquito and ant" refers to the style in which *nu shu*, is written; the latter is a now nearly extinct secret script used by Chinese women to correspond with one another. It possibly originated in the Soong Dynasty (900–1279) when women were denied a formal education and was "discovered" by an anthropologist in 1987. One reason for the difficulty in tracing the development of this language is the custom of burning a woman's books on her death so she might possess them in her afterlife.

"Translating Ancient Lines into the Vernacular." Triggering line: "When the line is crossed, contagion is produced." Catherine Clément (34). See above.

"The Downpour" quotes are from Sei Shōnagon, translator Ivan Morris, *The Pillow Book of Sei Shōnagon* (New York: Penguin, 1967).

Quotes in "Guard the Jade Pass" are from *The Immortal Sisters: Secrets of Taoist Women*, Thomas Cleary, editor and translator. Boston: Shambhala Publications, 1989.

"Tissue." Triggering line: "The imagination's cry is a sexual cry." Adrienne Rich.

"The New Calligraphy Tutor Is a Woman." Triggering line: "All laughter is allied with the monstrous." Catherine Clément (33). See above.

"Responding to Light" quotes from Luce Irigaray. "Body against Body: in relation to the mother," ("Le corps-à-corps avec la mère") in *Sexes and Genealogies* (New York: Columbia University Press, 1993), translated by Gillian Gill. Originally published in Paris: Les Éditions de Minuit, 1987.

Michelle Cliff. *The Land of Look Behind* (Ithaca: Firebrand Press, 1985).

"Sewing without Mother" quotes:
  Makoto Ueda quote fom "The Taxonomy of Sequence" in Earl Miner, ed., *Principles of Classical Japanese Literature* (Princeton: Princeton University Press, 1985), p. 90.
  Donald Keene quote from *Essays in Idleness: The Tsurezuregusa of Kenkō* (New York: Columbia University Press, 1967), p. xvi.